This book is to be returned on or before the last da

2RYa4

531

PINDER, BILL

FLIGHT AND FLOATING

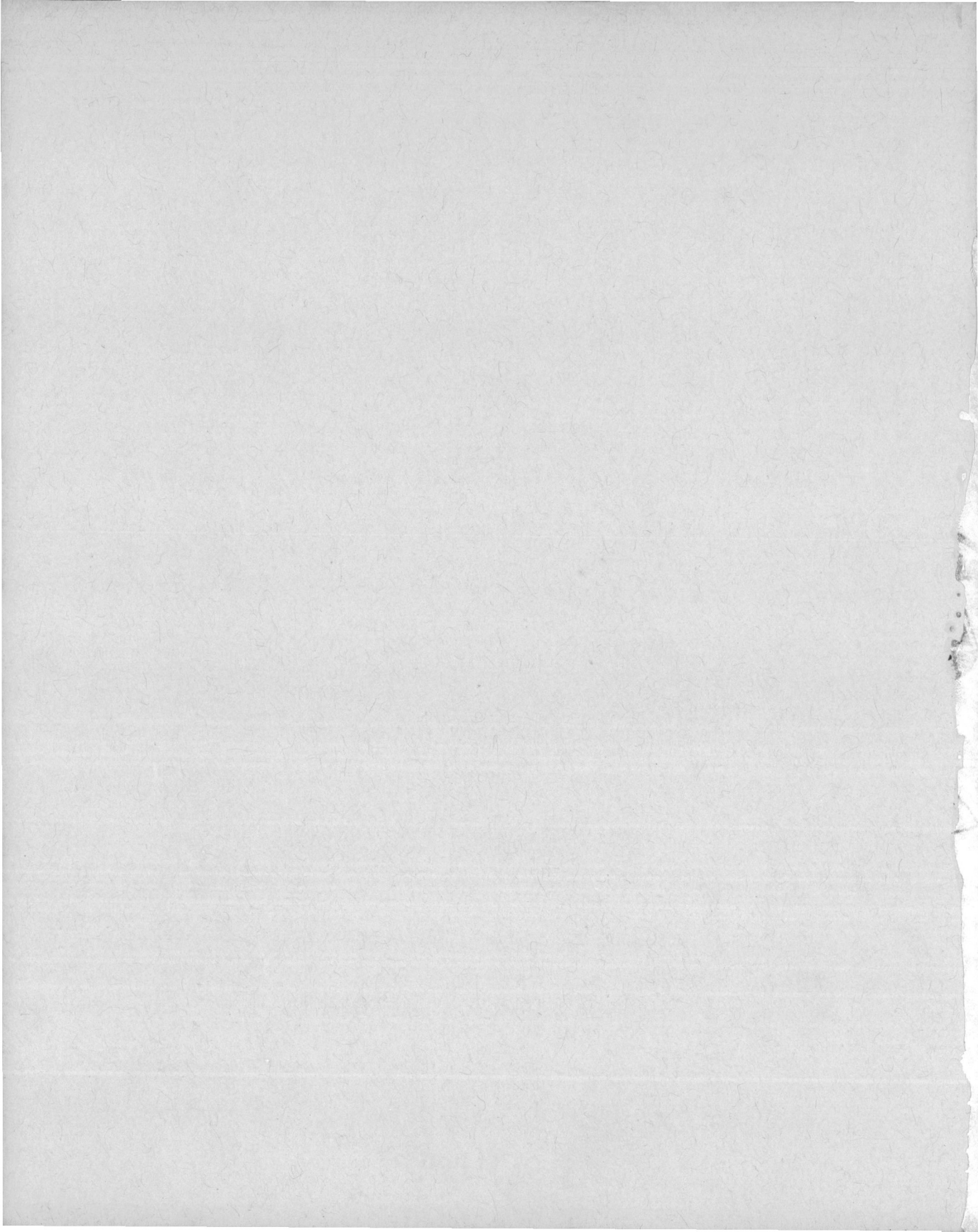

~ experiment · with ~

FLIGHT AND FLOATING

Bill Pinder

Illustrated by Leo Hartas

Designed by Steve Page
Edited by Mike Halson

Consultant: Geoff Puplett

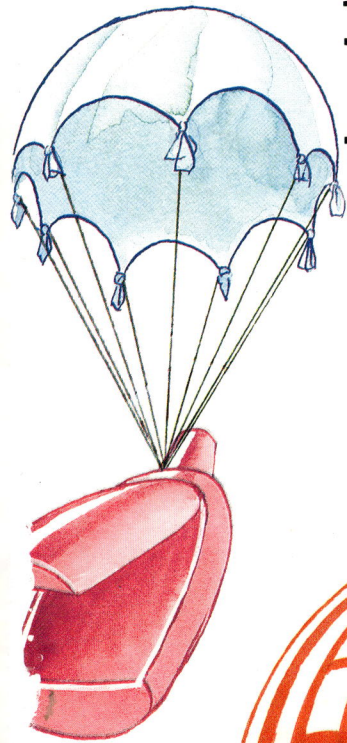

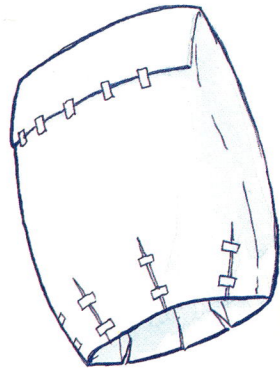

CONTENTS

British Library Cataloguing in Publication Data
Pinder, Bill
Experiment with flight and floating.
1. Science. Experiments using floating objects
2. Science. Experiments using flying objects
I. Title II. Hartas, Leo III. Series
507' 24
ISBN 0 00 191293 3
ISBN 0 00 190033 1 HB

William Collins Sons & Co Ltd
London · Glasgow · Sydney · Auckland
Toronto · Johannesburg

First Published in Great Britain 1989
© William Collins Sons & Co Ltd 1989

Printed in Great Britain by Cambus Litho, East Kilbride

ABOUT THIS BOOK

All through history, people have been fascinated by all the amazing things going on around them, and have been trying to find out why and how they happen.

This activity is called science, and the methods used to find things out are called experiments.

Over the centuries, scientists' experiments have helped to answer many questions about our world and the universe.

Because scientists take care to write down exactly what they did, other people can copy their work and find out important facts for themselves.

By doing the experiments in this book, you will find out for yourself how things float or fly. And at the same time, you will end up with lots of useful models too.

CHECKING WHAT YOU HAVE LEARNT

If you want to check what you have learnt, turn to pages 30 – 31. There, you will find reminders of the main science facts that can be found in this book.

EXPERIMENT TIMES

None of the experiments will take more than half a day. Making the models will take anything from a few minutes up to a couple of hours. You can easily guess how long you will need by reading through the instructions.

3

WHAT YOU WILL NEED

Each experiment tells you all the things you will need. Most of them can be found around the house. Everything else can be bought cheaply from high street stores.

Before you start experimenting, collect together the items you need for the experiments you want to do.

It's a good idea to keep the things you have used for an experiment – many of them will be useful again. You could build up a store of science materials and keep them together in a handy place.

SCIENCE WORDS

Some experiments have words which look like this: *centre of gravity*. Find out what they mean on page 31.

SCIENCE NOTEBOOK

You will find it useful to keep a special notebook to write down what you have done and found out. This will help you remember what happened. Use drawings as well as words.

IMPORTANT THINGS TO REMEMBER

Before you get started, remember that scientists always obey these golden rules:

1 Make sure everything is ready before you start work.

2 Choose a safe area in which to work. It needs to be somewhere where it doesn't matter if you make a mess. A worktop near a sink is a good idea.

3 Always take care about what you are doing. For an experiment to work, each step must be carried out according to the instructions.

4 Wear protective clothing, such as an apron or an old shirt.

5 Be very careful when using a sharp knife or scissors. Use a cutting board, not a worktop or table. Hold the object to be cut firmly, and cut away from your body, as shown in the picture.

5

SINK OR SWIM

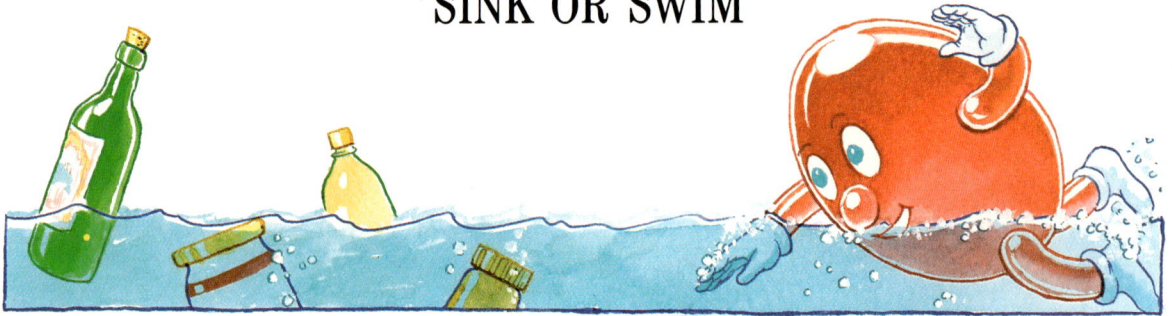

If someone asked you whether an object would float or sink in water, you may well be able to guess the right answer by feeling its weight.

For scientists, guesswork isn't enough. They need to know exactly what makes things sink or float. Find out more in this experiment.

You will need:
a jar with a screw-on top
some washing powder and damp sand
  (enough of each to fill the jar)
an elastic band
kitchen scales
a bucket full of water

1 Fill the jar three-quarters full with water and screw the top on. Put the jar into the bucket. Add water to the jar, or take some out, until it floats as shown in the picture.

2 Take the jar out of the water and pull on the elastic band to mark how high up the water comes.

3 Put the jar on to the scales. Write down how much it weighs.

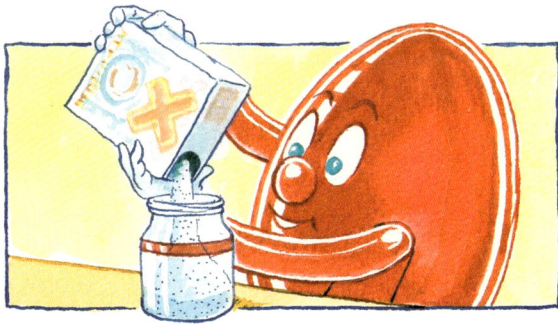

4 Dry the inside of the jar, then fill it up to the elastic band with washing powder. Screw on the top and put the jar into the water. Does it float better or worse than before?

5 Weigh the jar and write down the weight. Next, refill the jar up to the band with the sand and do exactly the same as with the washing powder.

What happens to the water level in the bucket when you put in the jar?

WHAT HAPPENED AND WHY?

water level rises

Each time you put the jar into the bucket, it pushed some water aside, making the water level in the bucket higher.

The jarful of water weighed only a bit less than the water it pushed aside.

The lightest filling was the washing powder. The jarful of washing powder weighed a lot less than the water pushed aside – and it floated really well.

water   washing powder   sand

The heaviest filling was the sand. The jarful of sand weighed more than the water pushed aside – and it sank.

So an object will float if it weighs less than the water it pushes aside. If it weighs more, it will sink.

MORE ABOUT FLOATING

Not all forms of water are the same. A litre of sea water will weigh more than river or tap water because of the dissolved salt it contains.

Usually, humans weigh more than the sea water they push aside, so they need to swim to stop themselves from sinking. But there is one place, called the Dead Sea, which is so full of salt that people can float in it quite comfortably.

A PLASTICINE BOAT

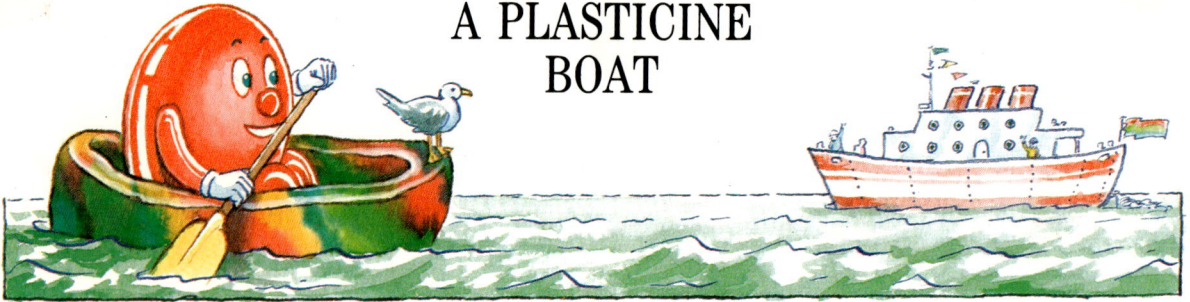

The experiment on pages 6 – 7 showed that objects sink if they are heavier than the water they push aside. If you dropped blocks of iron, steel or concrete into water, they would vanish without trace. Yet any of these can be made to float. This experiment shows you how it is done.

You will need:
an egg-sized lump of Plasticine
a small marble
a basin filled with water

1 Drop the lump of Plasticine into the basin. It will sink straight to the bottom.

2 Flatten out the Plasticine into a thin round pancake. Then make it into a bowl shape. Check there are no holes.

3 Gently put the Plasticine 'boat' into the water. It should float, but if it doesn't, try to improve the shape by making it thinner.

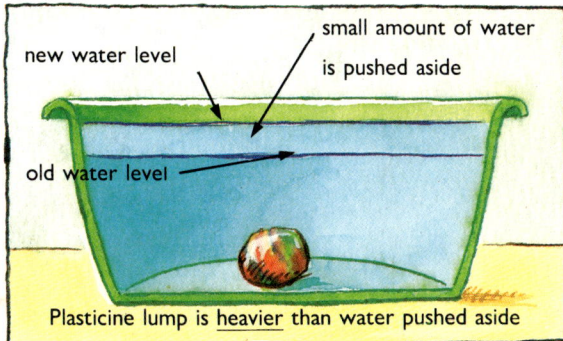

large amount of water is pushed aside

Plasticine boat is lighter than water pushed aside

4 Once the boat is floating properly, carefully put the marble into it. The boat should be able to carry it quite easily.

HOW DOES IT WORK?

This experiment shows that whether an object sinks or floats depends on its shape.

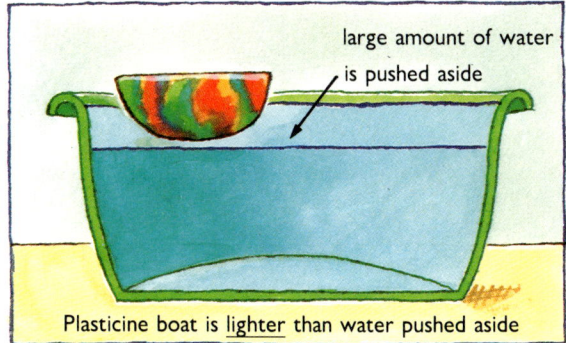

new water level

small amount of water is pushed aside

old water level

Plasticine lump is heavier than water pushed aside

When you put the Plasticine lump into the basin, it pushed aside only a small amount of water. The water weighed less than the Plasticine, so the Plasticine sank.

Then, when you made your boat, you changed the shape of the Plasticine. This time, much more water was pushed aside.

The boat now weighed less than the water it pushed aside. And what happened? It floated!

Almost any object can be made to float in the same way – by giving it the right shape.

THE FIRST IRON BOAT

Until the 18th century, all ships were made of reeds, animal skins or wood, which everyone knew would float. But in 1787 the first iron boat was built in Scotland.

Many people, including shipbuilders, were convinced that something so heavy would sink straight to the bottom. It didn't – and the age of iron ships had begun.

A MAGIC DIVER

How can you make something go up and down in the water at your command?

You will need:
the top of a ballpoint pen
some Plasticine
a clear plastic bottle with a screw-on cap
a jug of water

1 Make a Plasticine ball about the size of a small marble. Push the pen top through it as shown. Squeeze the Plasticine so that it holds firmly to the pen top.

This experiment explains how – and shows you a trick which will mystify your friends.

2 Place the diver in the jug of water. It should float, with just the very top above the surface. If not, add or take off Plasticine until it floats as shown in the picture.

3 Fill the bottle right to the top with water. Then, place the diver inside and screw the cap on tight. That's all you have to do!

4 To make the diver sink, squeeze the bottle. A hard squeeze will make it sink quickly, while a gentle squeeze will make it sink more slowly. Let go and the diver will rise again.

5 To amaze your friends, tell them that the diver will obey your instructions. Then tell it to sink and gently squeeze the bottle. Order it to rise, and let it go. Your friends will be baffled!

HOW DOES IT WORK?

When you put the diver in the bottle, a bubble of air was trapped inside. This bubble was just enough to keep it afloat.

Squeezing the bottle made the water press hard on the bubble. This made it smaller, and so it pushed aside less water.

The diver became a bit heavier, and it sank.

large air bubble

small air bubble

When you stopped squeezing, the bubble got bigger again, and up she came!

This trick was invented over 300 years ago by a Frenchman called René Descartes. Its proper name is the 'Cartesian diver'.

SUBMARINES

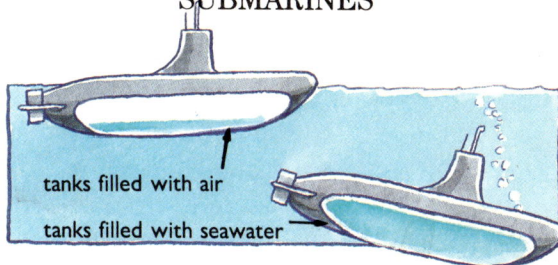

tanks filled with air

tanks filled with seawater

Submarines work in the same way as the diver – by changing the amount of air and water they contain. To dive, air is let out of special tanks, and they fill with water.

By carefully controlling the amount of air and water in the tanks, the submarine can be made to stay at any depth underwater.

When the submarine wishes to return to the surface, air is pumped back into the tanks, forcing the water back into the sea.

A PADDLE-BOAT

For centuries, the only way to make a boat move was to paddle it yourself or by using the wind.

Then, in 1783, the first boat to use an engine was built. The engine was used to turn a huge paddle wheel which churned through the water.

This experiment shows you how paddle-boats work.

You will need:
a piece of balsa wood, about 15 cm long, 5 cm wide and 1 cm thick
a craft knife
a junior hacksaw
a piece of stiff plastic (part of a large ice-cream container is ideal)
a thin elastic band about 6 cm long
a pencil
scissors
a bath or large basin filled with water

2 cm
3 cm

Mind your fingers!

1 Mark a shape on the balsa wood as shown. Cut out the shape, using the craft knife and the hacksaw.

2 Using the scissors, cut out a paddle from the piece of plastic, 2 cm long and 1 cm wide.

3 Twist the elastic band to make it half as long. Then, stretch it across the gap at the back of the boat. Push the paddle into place, as shown.

wind this way

4 Carefully wind up the paddle – about ten turns should do. Place the boat in the water and let go of the paddle. What happens?

WHAT HAPPENED AND WHY?

boat moves forwards
paddle unwinds and pushes against water

As the elastic band unwound, it made the paddle push against the water. This made the boat move forwards. The same happens when you walk, except that your feet are pushing against the ground.

OTHER THINGS TO DO

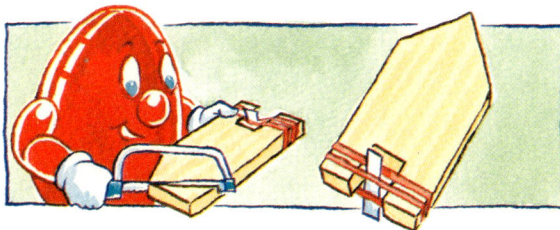

See if you can make your boat go faster and further. You could try:
● winding the paddle more times
● cutting a V-shape in the front of the boat
● using a different elastic band

If a friend makes a boat, you can have races.

PADDLES AND PROPELLERS

propeller spins and pushes against water

For about 50 years, all boats with engines were driven by paddles. Then, in 1836, a new invention came along – the screw propeller.

Screw propellers have a special shape. As they spin, they push against the water, just like the paddle in your boat.

'Rattler'   'Alecto'

There were many arguments about whether propellers were better than paddles. In the end, a tug-of-war was held, between the paddle-driven 'Alecto' and the propeller-driven 'Rattler'.

The 'Rattler' won, and ever since, most ships have had propellers. Paddle-boats are still found, though, mainly on rivers such as the Mississippi in the United States of America.

MAKING BOATS SAFE

When people take their boats out to sea, they need to know that they will not capsize (fall over sideways) if the water becomes rough.

This experiment looks at what makes some boats less likely to capsize than others.

You will need:
the balsa wood boat from the experiment
  on pages 12 – 13
a cheap ball-point pen
a lump of Plasticine
a bowl of water

1   Make a hole through the middle of the boat with the ball-point pen, as shown. The pen forms the boat's mast and should be held firmly in the hole.

2   Next, make a Plasticine sausage and wrap it around the bottom of the mast. Put the boat in the water and make waves with your hand. How does the boat behave?

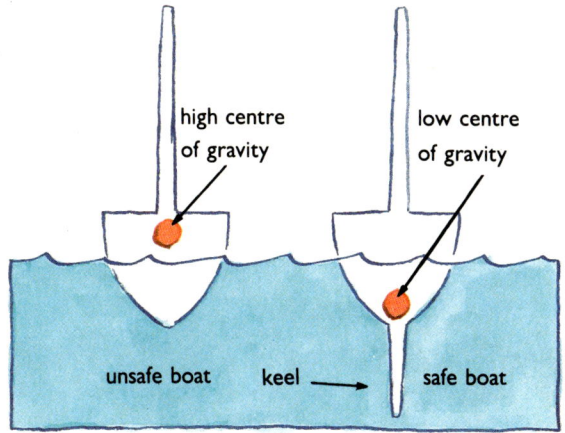

high centre of gravity

low centre of gravity

unsafe boat · keel → · safe boat

3 Now put the Plasticine about 1 cm higher and make more waves. What happens this time? Keep raising the Plasticine and making waves until you reach the top of the mast.

WHAT HAPPENED AND WHY?

The higher up the mast you put the Plasticine, the more likely the boat was to capsize.

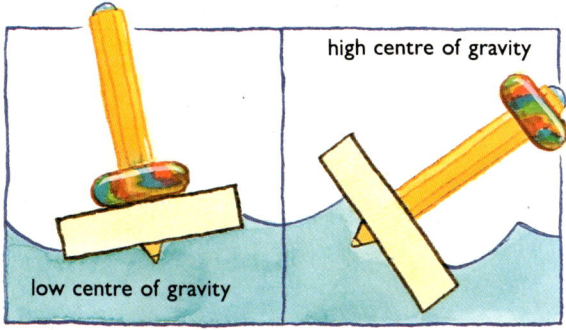

high centre of gravity

low centre of gravity

This is because you were raising its *centre of gravity*.

The centre of gravity is the point where an object balances. Every object has one. The higher the centre of gravity, the easier it is for thc object to topple over.

To make ships and boats safer, boat builders often lower the centre of gravity by putting a heavy weight below the water line. This is called ballast. Smaller boats have a keel (a large metal base) to do the same job.

MORE ABOUT CENTRES OF GRAVITY

The centre of gravity is important in all forms of transport, not just boats. Think of tall vehicles such as London's famous double-decker buses, for example. These have a very low centre of gravity, so they will not topple over even when they are filled with passengers.

A HOVERCRAFT

Many people think of hovercraft as a type of boat – because they are usually seen travelling across water.

But hovercraft are not really boats at all. Instead of moving through the water, they actually ride above it on a cushion of air.

Here's how to make a simple hovercraft of your own.

You will need:
a small polystyrene meat tray
a cork
some glue
a bicycle pump
a metal adaptor used to blow up footballs
a balloon
a craft knife
a thin knitting needle

Be very careful!

1 Cut a 1 cm thick piece off the cork with the craft knife. Then, using the knitting needle, make a small hole through the middle of the cork piece.

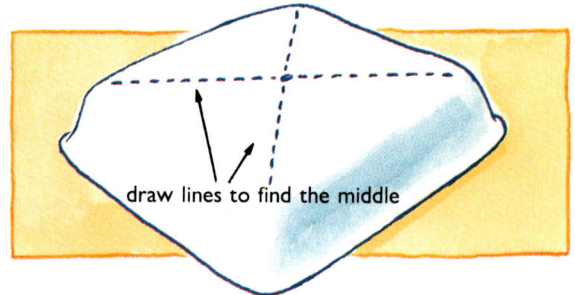

draw lines to find the middle

2 Turn the meat tray upside down and pierce a hole through the middle. Widen the hole a bit so it is very slightly bigger than the hole in the cork.

3 Glue the cork piece over the hole in the tray. Wait until the glue has dried.

4 Stretch the neck of the balloon over the cork piece. The hovercraft is now ready to fly.

5 Screw the adaptor to the bicycle pump and push it through the hole as shown. Pump up the balloon. Pull out the adaptor and place the hovercraft on a smooth surface.

6 The hovercraft should now float just above the surface. To check, give it a gentle push and it should slide easily along.

HOW DOES IT WORK?

As the balloon goes down, it forces air under the hovercraft. So much air becomes trapped between the surface and the hovercraft that the hovercraft is lifted up to make room.

As the hovercraft rises, most of the air escapes around the edges. To keep the hovercraft airborne would need a constant supply of air to be forced underneath.

A real hovercraft works in the same way. Huge fans pump air underneath the craft to lift it up, while giant propellers push it forward.

OTHER THINGS TO DO

Try to control the hovercraft's direction by blowing at it. Get a friend to make one too, so you can have races.

A PAPER HELICOPTER

If you drop a sheet of paper, it will not fall straight to the ground. Instead, it will flutter from side to side and land quite gently.

This happens because the paper is held up by the air as it falls. To find out more about how air affects falling objects, try making this model helicopter.

You will need:

a piece of paper about 20 cm long and 15 cm wide (cartridge paper or thin card is best)

a pencil and ruler

scissors

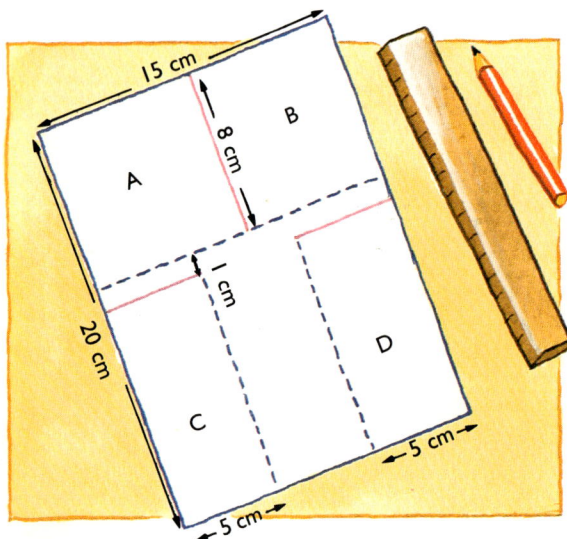

1 Mark out the paper as shown in the picture.

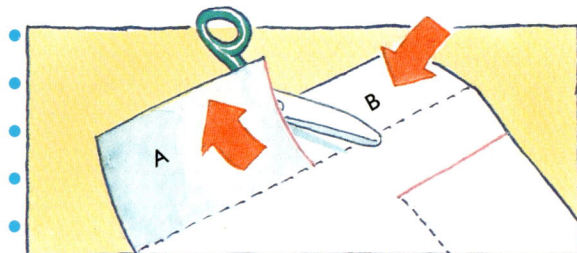

2 Cut along the lines shown in red with the scissors. Fold A forwards and B backwards. These folds are the helicopter's *rotors*.

3 Next fold C and D into the middle. Lastly, fold up a 2cm strip at the bottom. The helicopter is now ready to fly.

4 Find a high spot to drop the helicopter from, such as the top of the stairs or a balcony. Let it go and watch what happens.

After a few goes, try these tests: What happens if you make the rotors smaller? And if you straighten out rotor A but leave rotor B alone?

WHAT HAPPENED AND WHY?

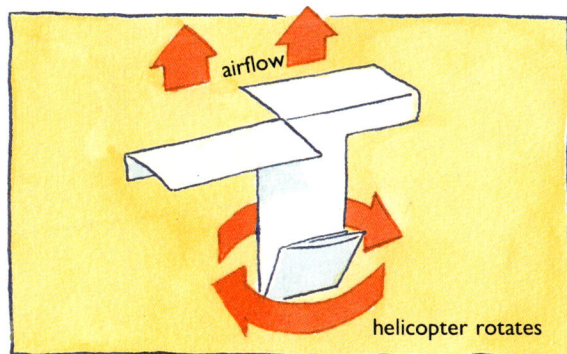

When you let go of the helicopter, it began to drop towards the ground. As it did so, air flowed rapidly past the rotors, making them rotate (spin round).

The flow of air above and below the rotors actually helped keep the helicopter up in the air. This effect is called *lift*.* The faster the rotors turned, the greater the lift.

In a real helicopter, powerful engines make the rotors turn dozens of times every second. This produces so much lift, the rotors can hold the helicopter up in the air.

SYCAMORE SEEDS

If you look closely at a sycamore seed, you will see that it is really a small round seed attached to a single rotor.

When the seeds drop from the tree, they rotate and stay in the air for quite a long time.

Falling in this way gives them a good chance of being carried by the wind to a spot well away from the tree's shade – where it is light enough for them to grow.

OTHER THINGS TO DO

If a friend makes a helicopter, you can have competitions to see whose can stay in the air the longest. Use crayons to decorate them – not felt-tipped pens or the ink will make them damp and floppy!

* See pages 20 – 21 and 22 – 23 for more about lift.

WHAT MAKES AEROPLANES FLY?

Have you ever wondered how planes are able to take off and rise up into the sky? You can find the answer by taking a close look at the wings.

Wings have a special shape, called *aerofoils*. This experiment shows how an aerofoil works.

You will need:
a sheet of thin card
a plastic drinking straw
some quick-drying glue
scissors
a small screwdriver
2 metres of cotton
a hair dryer

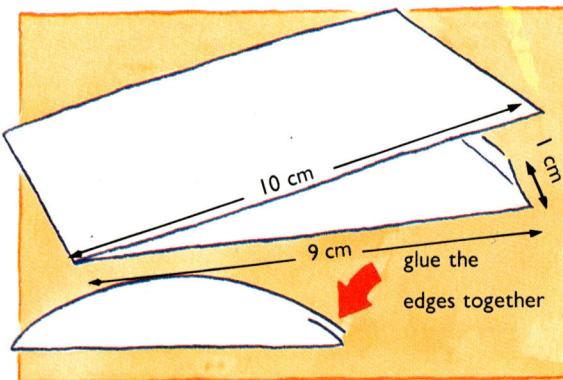

1 Cut out a piece of card 20 cm by 16 cm and fold as shown. Glue the edges together to make a wing.

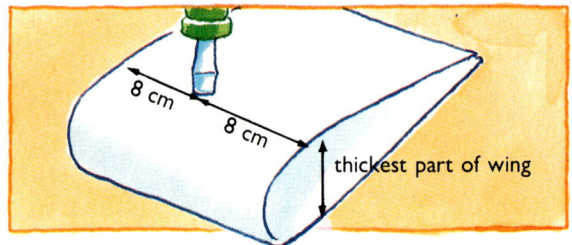

2 Use the screwdriver to pierce a hole right through the wing at the point shown in the picture. Make the hole just big enough to fit the drinking straw.

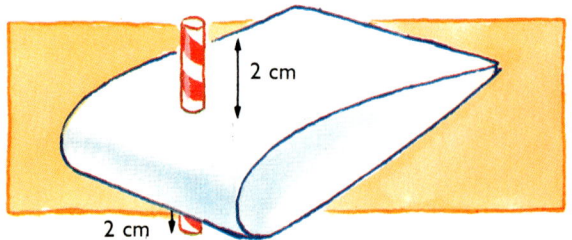

3 Push the straw through the card. Add some glue around the straw where it touches the card. When the glue is dry, trim the ends as shown.

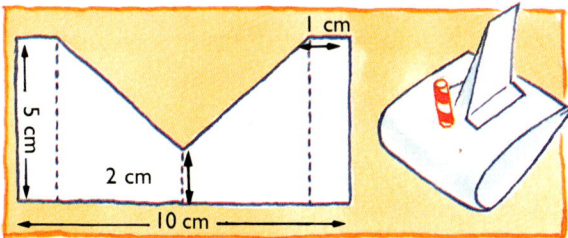

4 To make the tail fin, cut out and fold the piece of card as in the picture. Glue it to the wing.

5 Push the cotton through the straw and tie the ends to two chair legs. Aim the hair dryer at the wing and switch it on. The wing should rise up the cotton (you may need to help it at first).

HOW DOES IT WORK?

The wing moved upwards because of the way air pressed against it.

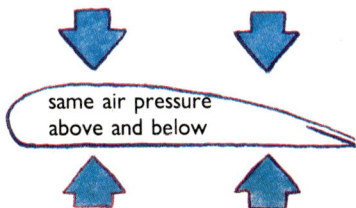

same air pressure above and below

When the air around the wing was still, it pressed against it with the same force from all directions. The *air pressure* above and below the wing was the same.

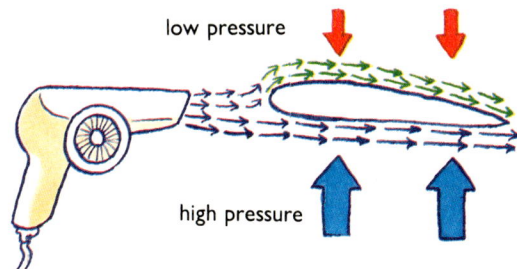

low pressure

high pressure

Switching on the hair dryer made air flow quickly past the wing. The air passing over the top had further to go to reach the other side than the air below it, so it moved faster.

A scientific law says that the faster air flows, the less the pressure becomes.

The air pressure pushing the wing down was now less than the pressure pushing the wing up. This produced what is called *lift*,* and the wing rose up.

Aerofoils only work when air flows past them quickly. That is why an aeroplane has to accelerate down the runway before it takes off.

Once it is moving very fast, there is enough lift to raise the whole plane into the sky.

* See pages 18 – 19 and 22 – 23.

flight·experiments

CONTROLLING AEROPLANES

How do pilots control their aeroplane? To answer this question, you first need one to experiment with.

You will need:
a piece of paper about 20 cm long and 15 cm wide
scissors

1 Place the paper on the table and fold one end back 1 cm.

2 Make three more folds, then fold the paper in half lengthways.

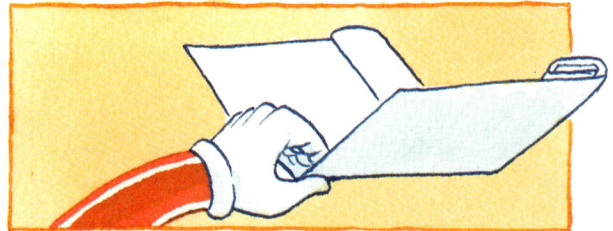

This plane is one of the simplest to make, but it is also one of the best fliers!

dips and swoops – add another fold

good flight path

dives – take out one fold

3 Hold the plane as shown and launch it gently into the air. It should fly at a shallow angle for a few metres. If not, make adjustments until it does.

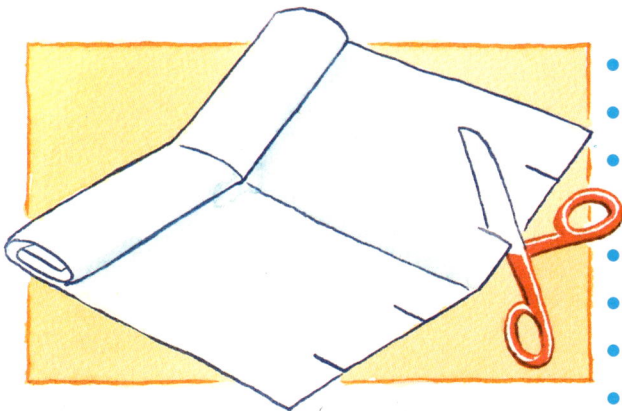

4 Give the plane wing flaps by making two small cuts, about 1 cm long and 4 cm apart, on the edge of each wing.

5 Fold up the flaps as shown, and see how they affect the way the plane flies. (You may need to make another fold at the front of the plane to get it to fly properly again.)

6 Try putting the flaps in different positions: a) both fully up; b) both fully down; c) both half-way up; d) one up and one down.

WHAT HAPPENED AND WHY?

The experiment on pages 20 – 21 shows

how a wing's shape affects the way air flows over it.

The same goes for the whole of an aeroplane. The flaps you made changed the shape of your plane and made it fly in different ways.

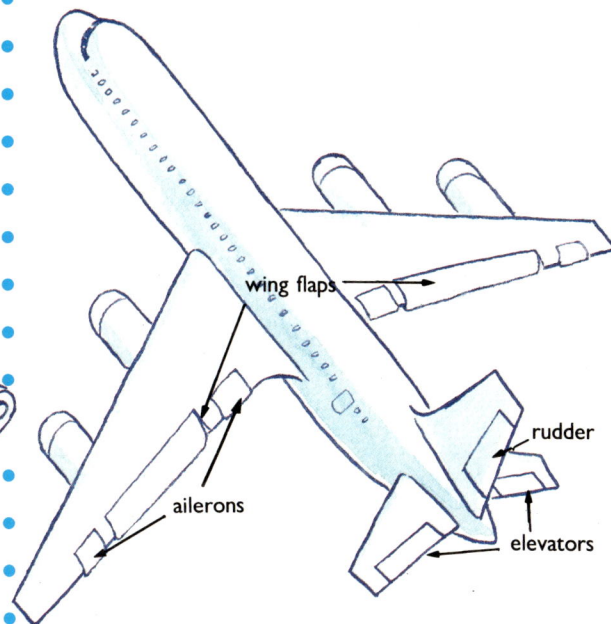

A real plane is controlled by four types of flap:
- wing flaps increase or reduce *lift* (see pages 20 – 21). They are mainly used when landing or taking off.
- ailerons turn the plane by making one wing go up and the other go down.
- elevators raise or lower the plane's nose, making it point up, down or straight ahead.
- the rudder helps steer the plane to the left or the right.

A HOT AIR BALLOON

Hot air balloons were the first working flying machines. They are still common today all over the world.

You will need:
a large, lightweight plastic bag – either a
  bag from a dry cleaner's or a dustbin
  liner
sticky tape
a fan heater or a hair dryer

Remember that plastic bags and electrical equipment can be dangerous. Check with a grown up that it is OK for you to do this experiment.

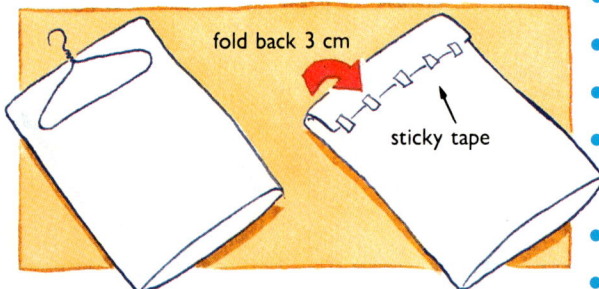

fold back 3 cm

sticky tape

1 If you are using a dry cleaning bag, seal the end where the coat hanger goes, using the sticky tape. Make sure the seal is fairly airtight.

This experiment shows you how to make your own hot air balloon and explains how they work.

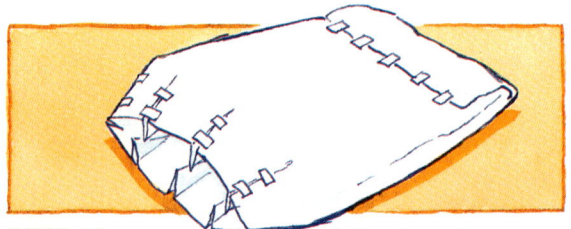

2 Narrow one end of the bag by making some tucks and sticking them down with the tape. The balloon is now ready to fly.

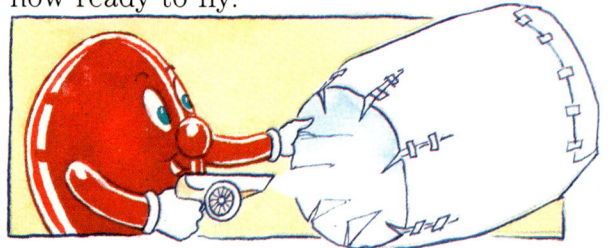

3 Choose a room with as high a ceiling as possible. The balloon will work best if the room is cool. Switch on the fan heater or hair dryer and hold the bag so the hot air goes inside.

Don't hold too close or the bag might melt.

4 When there is plenty of hot air inside the bag, let it go. It should rise slowly upwards. If it topples over, add extra sticky tape at the bottom to weigh it down and try again.

HOW DOES IT WORK?

The balloon rose up because of the way air changes when it is heated.

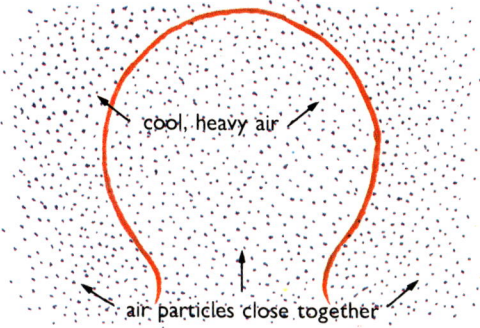
cool, heavy air
air particles close together

Air is made up of countless tiny particles which can move around freely. When the air is heated, it expands – which means the tiny particles move further apart.

The picture shows the balloon filled with cool air. The air particles were close together, and the air was quite heavy. The weight of the plastic bag kept the balloon on the floor.

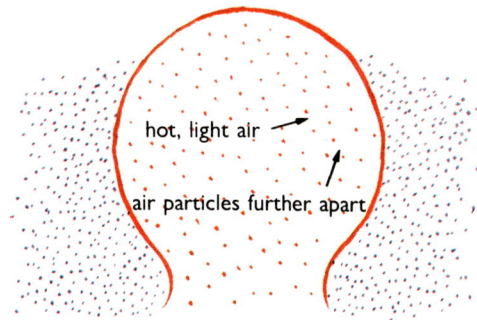
hot, light air
air particles further apart

Now look what happened when the cool air was replaced by hot air. Because there were not so many air particles in the balloon, the air was much lighter.

Even with the weight of the plastic bag, he balloon was now so light, it floated up to the ceiling.

As the air in the balloon cooled, it became heavy again, and the balloon sank to the floor.

MORE ABOUT HOT AIR BALLOONS

People have known for a very long time that hot air rises. Some claim that a 5000-year-old picture found in Egypt shows a hot air balloon made from paper.

The first balloon to carry passengers flew in France in 1783. On board were a duck, a sheep and a cockerel!

Shortly afterwards, two men flew several kilometres over the French capital, Paris. Their flight was very dangerous, since the fire they used to heat the air also kept setting the balloon alight!

25

A KITE

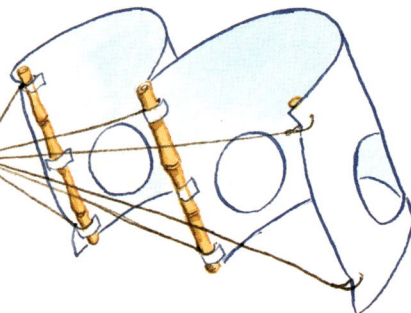

Most home-made things that fly cannot be controlled. They only spend a few seconds in the air before returning to earth.

Kites are different – they can be controlled even when they are high up in the sky. To find out how they work, the best thing to do is to make one!

You will need:
a large, strong plastic bag – a dustbin liner
  is ideal
three thin garden canes at least 1
  metre long
some sticky tape
30 metres of strong fishing line
scissors
a saucer
a junior hacksaw

fold into four

2 Fold the sheet as shown. Then, mark a circle round the saucer using the point of the scissors.

1 Cut off the bottom of the bag. Next, cut down one of the edges to form a large plastic sheet.

3 Push the scissors through the plastic and carefully cut out the circle. You should end up with four holes in the sheet.

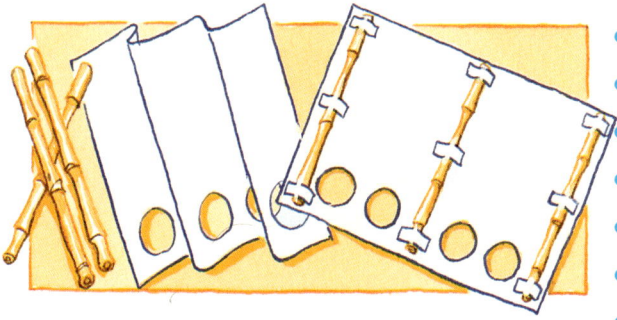

4 Use the hacksaw to cut the canes to the size shown. Then, fix them in place with the sticky tape – one at each end and one in the middle.

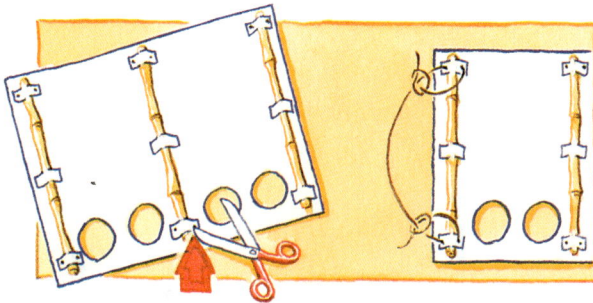

5 Make 12 holes in the plastic sheet with the scissors, as in the picture. Next, cut three two-metre lengths of fishing line. Thread them through the holes and tie them in place.

6 Fold the kite as shown and tie on the rest of the fishing line. The kite is now ready to fly.

wind

7 Fly the kite in a wide open space on a day with at least a little wind. First, ask a friend to hold the kite. Then, walk ten metres away into the wind, unwinding the line as you go.

Tell your friend to open up the kite and hold it in the air. To help the kite fly upwards, try walking away from it. As it rises, let out more line.

HOW DOES IT WORK?

The kite is pushed up into the sky by a flow of air – in other words, the wind! The line stops it blowing away.

You can use the line to control how high the kite flies and how long it stays in the air.

How high do you think you could get your kite to fly? The world record for a single kite is over 8,500 metres, almost as high as Mount Everest!

PARACHUTING TO SAFETY

Parachutes are a good way of dropping to the ground in safety. As well as carrying people, they can also be used for all kinds of objects such as space rockets.

You will need:
a clean, empty plastic shampoo bottle
  with a screw-on top
scissors
a junior hacksaw
some string
a dinner plate (see step 3)
a felt-tip pen
six pieces of cotton, each 30 cm long
a small, thin plastic bag (the kind
  supermarkets use for small items)
two elastic bands, tied together

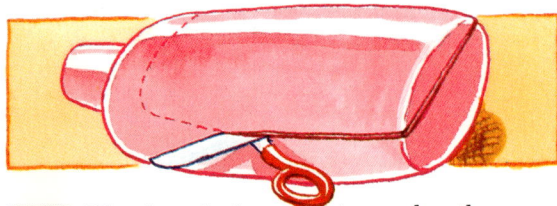

1 The bottle is used to make the rocket. Using the scissors, cut the bottle into two as shown. You may need to use the hacksaw to cut through the bottom.

The parachute in this experiment is attached to a home-made rocket, which you can fire into the air yourself.

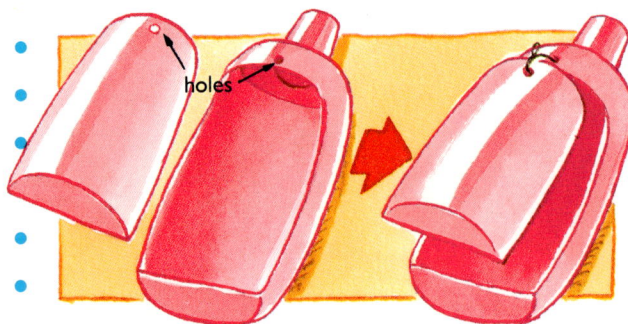

holes

2 Pierce holes in the two pieces and make a string loop as shown. The 'flap' should open and close freely.

3 Now make the parachute. Cut the plastic bag into a single sheet as shown. Draw a large circle on the sheet, using the plate, and cut it out.

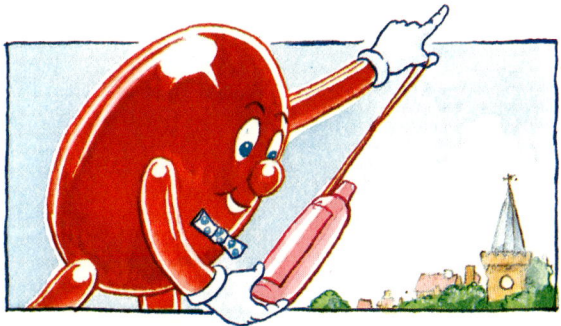

4 Use the scissors to pierce six holes where shown and attach the pieces of cotton. Tie the ends into a knot.

5 Remove the bottle top and push the knotted end of the cotton through the bottle neck from inside. Screw the top back on, to hold the cotton in place.

6 Unscrew the bottle top slightly and position the elastic bands as shown. Screw the cap down tightly so the elastic is held firmly.

7 Place the parachute inside the rocket and put the flap in position. Hold the rocket as shown and launch it into the air.

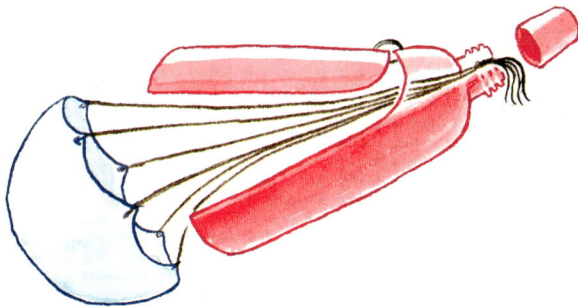

WHAT HAPPENED AND WHY?

As the rocket reached the highest point of its flight, the flap will have opened, releasing the parachute. The parachute lets the rocket fall gently to the ground.

air pushes upwards as it tries to escape

When most things fall towards the ground, the air easily moves out of the way. But parachutes have a special umbrella shape which traps air inside.

As it tries to escape, the air presses upwards, pushing the parachute back the way it has come. The push is not strong enough to stop the parachute falling, but it does slow it down.

WHAT DO YOU KNOW ABOUT FLIGHT AND FLOATING?

These two pages show the main science facts you can find out about in the experiments.

Any solid object can be made to float by giving it the right shape.

Boats with engines use paddles or propellers to push against the water.

An object will float if it weighs <u>less</u> than the water it pushes aside.

Boats need a low centre of gravity to stop them capsizing.

An object will sink if it weighs <u>more</u> than the water it pushes aside.

Submarines can stay at any depth, depending on how much water is in their tanks.

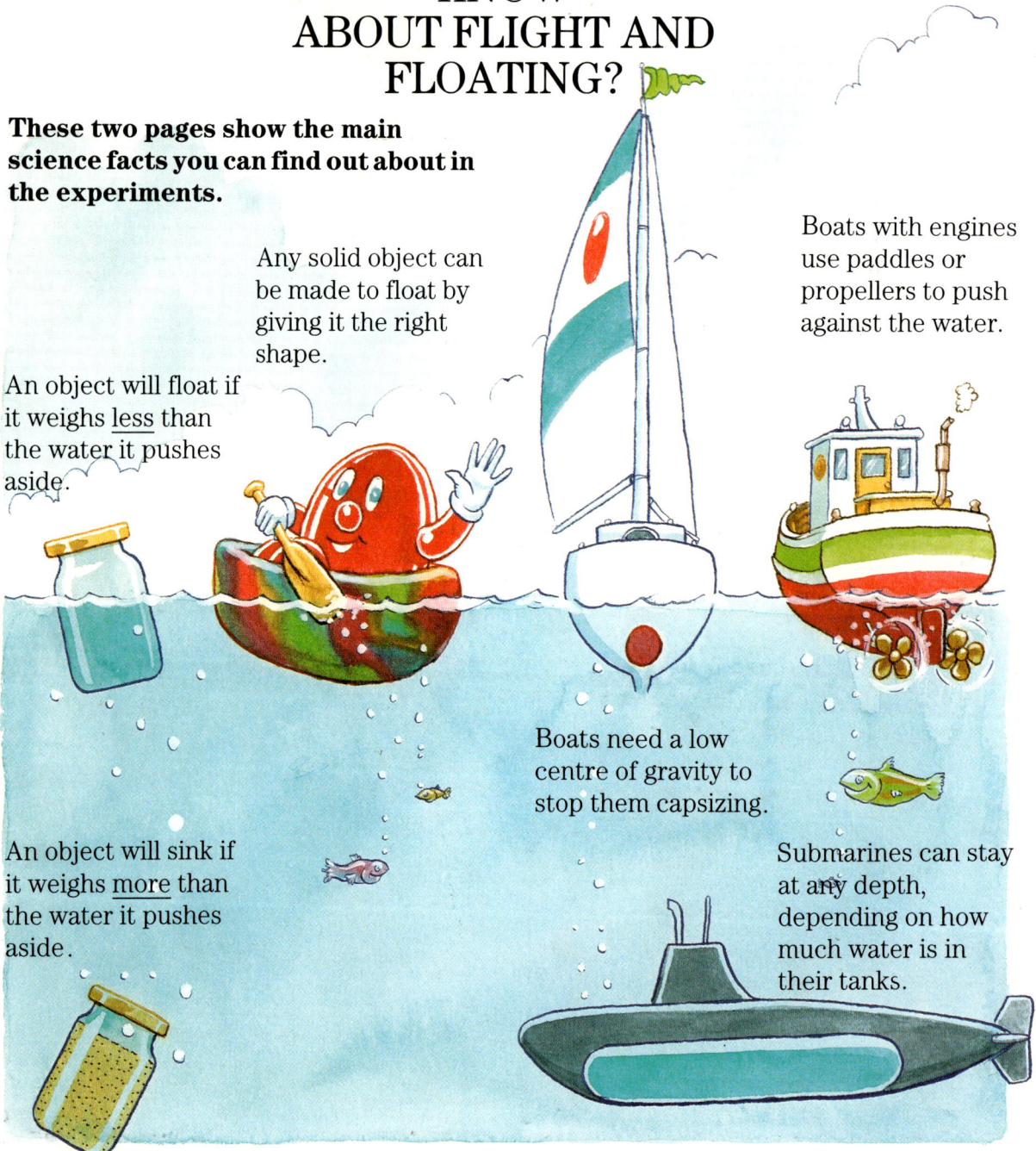

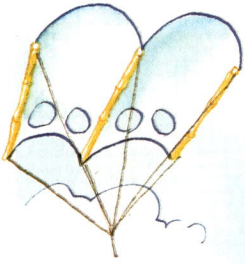

Kites are pushed up into the air by the wind.

Hot air balloons contain air which is lighter than the air outside.

Air flowing past a paper helicopter makes it rotate and produces *lift*.

Aeroplanes are lifted into the air by their aerofoil wings.

Hovercraft travel on a cushion of air.

The air trapped in parachutes makes them fall slowly.

Aeroplanes are controlled by their wingflaps, ailerons, elevators and rudder.

SCIENCE WORDS

Aerofoil
A special shape used in wings to affect the way air flows and produce lift.

Air pressure
The force produced by air pressing against something. Usually, the air pressure is the same in all directions.

Centre of gravity
The centre of gravity is the point where an object balances. The lower the centre of gravity, the harder it is to make the object fall over.

Lift
A force pushing an object upwards. Lift is produced when air flows past an aerofoil.

Rotors
Rotors are the part of a helicopter which go round and carry it into the air. They have an aerofoil shape, and produce lift when they turn.

31

Index